How to Hire the Right Estate Planning Attorney at a Fair Price

A Consumer's Guide to Finding the Right Attorney, at the Right Value, to Create Your Plan to Protect Your Money and Make Things Easy on Your Family

R. KELLEN BRYANT

Estate Planning Attorney

ISBN-10: 1500657166
ISBN-13: 978-1500657161

DEDICATION

This book is dedicated to my beautiful bride, Megan.

CONTENTS

DISCLAIMER (Lawyers will be lawyers.)

I hope that you find some interesting and useful information in this book. After you read, take notes, and go through your search process, the decision about whom you hire in the end will be YOURS! While I hope that this book will serve as a guide to narrow down your search, I cannot guarantee that you will ultimately decide to hire the right estate planning attorney. There is no ONE way to make a buying decision about anything, including a lawyer. That means that the information in this guide is not foolproof, but I do believe it will put you at least one step ahead of where you started.

PREFACE

There is much mystery surrounding what estate planning attorneys do and why you can get a HUGE range of potential price quotes. Estate planning can be quite a big decision, much like buying a car. Most people know how to price out and research cars, but most people do not know how to choose an estate planning lawyer. This book will teach you the difference between a "Yugo" estate plan and a "Rolls Royce" estate plan.

I not only based this book on conversations with attorneys, clients, and other folks the Northeast Florida area; I have discussed estate planning practice and procedures with many attorneys out of my region. I love to inquire how other attorneys run their practices, or hear stories about estate planning disasters. I am a part of multiple national estate planning attorney networks and local estate planning attorney networks. We can discuss trends and planning disasters via email lists.

After working with 500 families, and growing, I have had the opportunity to review the estate planning work of many other attorneys. My clients have either moved into town or otherwise left their attorney. I usually ask about the previous attorney and why they've come to me. Most importantly, I get to review the work of other attorneys.

Let me tell you… The documents are NOT all the same. I've seen trusts that are 8 pages, and I've seen trusts that have 90 pages.

I have written this book hopefully to allow you to digest it in one sitting, maybe over the weekend. You could take notes, but you should read it quickly. Then, find an estate planning attorney to hire to complete this important part of your financial planning and to protect you, your family, and your assets.

When you are finished with the book and select an attorney, give this book to a close friend and tell them to get their affairs in order! Most people want to do this type of planning, but they do not know how to get started or they're anxious about the unknowns.

Good luck with your planning. You made a prudent choice to read this book.

1. WHY BOTHER WITH ESTATE PLANNING?

Why Read This Book?

This book is for a person who wants to take care of their family and protect them from financial pitfalls, family fights, and the stress of dealing with financial issues related to death and incapacity. This book is not for somebody who just wants to get something easy, cheap, and simple.

In fact, this book will explain the perils that you can face when you want (or you think) estate planning that is cheap, easy, and simple.

Surprisingly, most people think that their family planning situation is easy. They think they need something basic. You will learn in this book, however, that family dynamics are not always easy and neither are your assets. Don't discount your family and financial situation as needing an easy plan, a cheap attorney, or a simple document found on the internet. In this book, you will find that there are many estate planning options out there and that attorneys are not just selling an expensive piece of paper. In reality, you pay an attorney for advice on how to make it easy on your family during your incapacity and after death. The documents are a way to define your plans. Everything will come together as long as you're properly educated about your estate planning options, and you know the difference between a good and bad attorney who will advise you about your plan.

I use the term "estate planning" to mean the creation of a will, trust, durable power of attorney, healthcare directives, and living will to set forth your instructions on how you would like your financial and physical needs managed during your incapacity and after death. Many people think "estate planning" only applies to families with millions of dollars. This is not true. "Estate" does not mean "millionaire." As a matter of fact, estate planning pro bono (for the public good; without charge) clinics are consistently held to assist low-income families with setting up their health directives.

Why Do You Need An Estate Plan?

Let's talk about why you need an estate plan. You need an estate plan for the same reason that airplane flight attendant tells you that, in case of an emergency landing, you must put an oxygen mask on your own face before securing the masks of your child or a loved one. You're not able to take care of others if you don't properly take care of yourself and take care of your planning. Just like in an airplane, you need to take care of your own planning and make sure you do everything right because planning ahead of death or incapacity allows you to take care of others. Ultimately, the most common reason families want to do estate planning is to make things easy for their family and avoid potential headaches and problems.

Making sure you do estate planning right should be of your utmost concern and this book will teach you how to hire the right person to help you plan correctly. The final and complete goal of an effective estate plan is to define what you want to happen if you lose competency or pass away. You must educate yourself on how to define your plans by reading books such as this one, or any other materials provided by attorneys in your area whom you may wish to hire. Attorneys should provide you with information when you first call to help you understand what options are out there, and how those options work.

From there, you can schedule your first meeting with an attorney and say, "Hey I've learned what about this from you and here's what I'm thinking about my estate plan. Here's where I'm having problems and concerns. Can you define this final result where I want x, y, and z to happen?"

What Goals Can I Have For My Estate Plan?

While this is not a comprehensive list1, I want to give you a

---

[1] I have resources with further detail on my website www.kellenbryantlaw.com

quick overview of the critical objectives an estate planning attorney can help you accomplish beyond "who gets what" and "who does what":

Probate. A long, cumbersome court process that is required when someone passes away with assets held individually. By "individually" held assets, I mean that one name is on an account, and there is no beneficiary. Another common individually held asset is your house. Most couples in their first marriage have joint accounts, and this is not a major issue; however, probate becomes an issue after the death of the first spouse.

An estate planning attorney can help you navigate through either avoiding probate or making sure that the probate process goes smoothly. Some families may want to use the probate court to make sure your family plays fair (the judge plays referee). Probate fees and costs generally run about 3-5% of the total estate value.

Guardianship. Probate is the most common thing that people want to avoid as a court proceeding; however, most people know little about guardianship. Guardianship is typically a much more expensive version of probate.

A guardianship is a probate during your lifetime when you do not have the capacity to manage your money. Most guardianship clients hate the process. Guardianship happens if you have poor estate planning, outdated estate planning documents, family fighting, no estate planning, or you're stubbornly maintaining control of your assets when you are no longer capable of doing so properly. The fees associated with a guardianship can exceed tens of thousands of dollars. Multiple attorneys get involved. Multiple medical professionals get involved. Some states require a jury to be involved. A proper estate planning attorney will have the documents and planning in place in order for you to avoid guardianship.

Catastrophic Injury and Mental Incapacity Protection. An estate planning attorney will help walk you through the medical choices that you will need to make if you were in a permanent, persistent vegetative state or end-stage terminal condition and you can't communicate your wishes. You will make decisions beforehand in order to avoid forcing your family to make difficult decisions and guesses about what you would have wanted. You can also direct your care if you are ever mentally incapacitated, such as having dementia. The estate planning attorney helps you define the care result that you desire under these circumstances.

Remarriage Protection. Are you concerned that your spouse will remarry after you're gone? Do you trust your spouse not to disinherit your children after you're gone? Do you currently have step-children? Are you looking to get married and you have kids from a previous marriage? Florida law, for example, is set to benefit the surviving spouse as a default, and the law does not want to leave a surviving spouse without anything. According to Florida law, your children can be disinherited through the actions of your spouse after you pass without a will, trust, and/or marriage agreement. Remember, a lot of times spouses get joint accounts together. Your spouse can do whatever he or she wants with the account after you're gone, which includes not giving it to your children when your spouse passes. Without the advice of an attorney to make sure everything is set up correctly, you could unintentionally disinherit your children.

Asset Protection From Creditors For You, Your Kids, and/or Your Spouse. Your estate plan can be set up to avoid protection from creditors during your lifetime, and/or for your children after your death. You might be thinking, "I don't owe anyone any money right now." But sometimes creditors can come out of the woodwork. Frivolous lawsuits can happen after a simple fender bender. If you own a business or you are a professional in a professional practice, a judgment creditor or lawsuit can appear at a moment's notice. It is important to know how you can protect yourself from this. You can also create asset protection for your spouse and kids to protect their assets if they're in an automobile accident and they have personal injury attorneys breathing down their necks. You can even structure your estate to protect your assets from other creditors, including nursing homes.

Spendthrift In-law and Divorce Protection. Another legal loss that an estate planning attorney can help you with is protection against your children's spendthrift spouses, who could potentially spend the money that you intend for your children or grandchildren to inherit. If you're also worried about your children potentially getting a divorce, this will protect your inheritance from being part of a divorce. Sometimes after receiving an inheritance, beneficiaries may co-mingle or put the money in their joint accounts with their spouse. That money is usually split if they get a divorce. You need to consider avoiding that area of loss and building provisions into your estate plan.

Simplicity, Harmony, and Values. You can pretty much voice any of your wishes in your estate plan. The only basic limitations are directives against common public policy and decency. For example, you can't put in there "you have to divorce that no good son in law of mine to get your inheritance." However, you can set up your estate to say, "Before my kids get their hands on the money they have to do x, y, and z." Examples of x, y, and z could be (x) get a full-time job, (y) graduate from college, and/or (z) no longer be in debt of their own. This would create a "no free ride" policy for a person.

Special Needs Children. If you have a child with special needs, then you'll learn from an estate planning attorney that you don't have to disinherit that child for fear that they will lose public benefits for their care. With a proper estate planning attorney, you can protect those benefits.

Inheritance Taxes. An estate planning attorney with a tax background can help you to avoid inheritance taxes (estate, gift, generation-skipping on both federal and state levels). Inheritance taxes are taxes paid on transfers of money that you have already paid income tax on! That's a form of double taxation. An estate planning attorney can help guide you through avoiding and reducing those costs.

Pets. Believe or not you may want to consider planning for your pets. Especially if you have a sweet spot for them or if you have pets with longevity that could easily exceed your own, such as horses, birds, or turtles.

Business Succession Planning. If you own a business, your business needs an estate plan. You can work with an estate planning attorney to create a contingency plan if you pass away while your business is running. Who is going to take over? How is it going to be run? Who will make sure the maximum values of the business are set up for your beneficiaries if they were faced with running the business in your absence? An estate planning attorney helps.

Obscure Asset Classes. You may have assets that are not conventional, such as a mortgage you are holding for somebody else (i.e. you are playing "bank"). You may own gold, yachts, airplanes, interest in airplanes, commercial real estate, rental property, timeshares, and so forth. Those are not common, as compared to typical banking like money market accounts, CDs, stocks and bonds, life insurance and annuities. You need to plan for those so that your beneficiaries will have a smooth transition of ownership of those assets if something happens to you.

Long-Term Care Asset Protection Planning. Believe it or not there are things you can do right now that do not involve long-term care insurance that protect your assets from a nursing home. A proper estate attorney can show you what to do and how to set up your estate to reduce that potential liability from your estate.

Avoid Double Probate. If you own real estate in a state other than where you currently live, your estate will also have to be probated in that other state. That's just ratcheting up the costs and expenses of the probate. Proper estate planning can help you avoid this.

The above listed are just a few examples of things that an estate planning attorney can incorporate into your estate planning to protect against legal losses. Some of these are mentioned in further detail throughout other chapters of this book.

Above all, proper estate planning will provide protection against court expenses due to arguments over your estate. Arguments can arise from inadequate legal drafting or imprecise legal language in your will or trust. Arguments can also arise from not thoroughly considering family situations and personalities. Many families have a member who has a dependency issue, substance abuse issue, entitlement issue, or may be argumentative with other members of the family. Because of this, other family members can experience problems and distress. As you'll learn in the next chapter, not just any attorney or any estate plan can protect you or your family from the distress of these arguments.

2. YOU GET WHAT YOU ASK FOR

Many people know Walmart as a place you go for low prices. Well, there are some people out there who are the equivalent to Walmart. They charge the lowest price, and they cut corners to do so. By charging the lowest price, they are not able to provide the type of service that you might get when you pay for a product that is custom-made at a higher price. They do this because they get plenty of calls asking, "How much for a will?"

Some things are worth buying at the lowest price, but legal advice is not something you want to pinch pennies over. This chapter will explain the pitfalls of looking for stating your terms.

The "cheapest" anything is problematic because that person is likely using the "wills and trust" practice area as a "loss leader." A loss leader is a business term, in which a business offers a product that is not profitable to them in the short term. The only reason they offer the product or service is to build their customer base and get them to spend more money in the future. In this case, a person offers a cheap will or trust because they hope to get future business from you or your family. In a minute, I will explain how this works.

Someone offering the cheapest estate planning might be an individual, or large business that spends a great deal of money on advertising, and they might "throw in" estate planning as a legal practice area for free. I know of someone in my area who does not charge any fee at all to prepare a will. Of course, that is why many people call the person.

Could My Free or Inexpensive Will Be a Loss Leader?

Imagine that you look in the phone book or Google, call around, and try to find the lowest price because you think, "I just want a basic will." You may not know what you will get when you pay for that lowest price. (That is hopefully why you're reading this book.) For a moment, let's compare this strategy to car shopping. Do you call around and look for the cheapest car? Probably not, or else we would only see Ford Pintos on the road.

Eventually, you'll reach the cheapest law office, and they might say, "We do a will for free." When you agree to work with them, they will proceed to ask you some basic questions like "Who do you want to be in charge if you die?" and "Who gets what?" They will collect the information and simply plug it into a form document that they use for hundreds, maybe even thousands of people. This is very similar to what you could do yourself on the internet, which I'll talk more about in the chapter three.

You will get the same form as everyone else and very little advice from an attorney before the product is complete. The attorney's assistant might do most of the work and just plug those names into the same template form that they use for everyone else. This is a problem because everyone has different and unique family circumstances and financial situations. (See chapter four about the Perfect Planning Triangle.)

Read the following two examples and decide if you think the same documents should be used for each person:

Person A. 77 years old, widow with potential health issues, $100,000 IRA, house that is paid off, and $200,000. Two adult children, one of whom is an alcoholic.

Person B. 38 years old. Married. Two children ages 10 and 4. House with a mortgage. Life insurance policies that payout one million dollars after the death of the second spouse.

I hope after comparing Person A with Person B, you see the different family situations, money situations, health situations, and needs.

Let's say you go ahead and set your final appointment with the person and you look the will over. Do you know what you are looking for beyond the correct spelling of names and who gets what? Few people without a law degree do, which is why you decided to call an attorney in the first place. The language on the document will be simple.

"I put this person in charge."

"These people get what's left over."

After the signing of your free will, the person will say something to the effect of, "I will hold onto the original copy of the will for you in case somebody wants to rip it up or thwart your wishes." The person will keep the original and will give you a photocopy. You will likely have no reason to question whether or not this practice makes sense for you and your family.

Right now that might sound like exactly what you want; a basic will for a free, or low price. The person safely holds onto the original will, so you don't need to worry about it. However, realize this: in order for this person to make a living, money has to come from somewhere. What they have probably provided is a loss leader for their business. The person will not spend much of his or her time with you, and many important elements of your will could be left out, which will conveniently provide more profitable business for the person in the future.

Perhaps this person in my example did not give you a durable power of attorney, healthcare surrogate designation, and living will. If you were to get in a car accident or develop dementia, Parkinson's, or any other long-term illness, you may not be able to manage your finances or make healthcare decisions for yourself. In order for a relative or friend to manage your finances and make healthcare decisions for you, that person will need to go get a court guardianship, which costs $5,000 at minimum. $10,000 in fees and costs are very likely.

In this situation, the person who needs to make healthcare decisions for you is likely to seek help from the same attorney who did your will, but who didn't tell you about avoiding this problem. The attorney will gladly handle the guardianship, which will end up costing your family tens of thousands of dollars. What did that "free" will in my example cost you? It cost you about $10,000. While it was free for you in the beginning, the person used it as a loss leader to possibly charge you much higher in the future.

What Else Could Be Left Out of a Free or Cheap Will?

There are many provisions that an attorney can, and should, include in a comprehensive estate plan to prevent monetary loss down the road. I discussed many of these in the first chapter, including avoidance of probate, which can be an expensive legal process. More information is also given in chapter seven, where I describe many sub-categories of estate planning.

Let's go back to my example of the "Penny-Pincher" attorney. When you pass away, your family will find the photocopy of your will, and guess who they will need to go to for the original? The attorney who drafted the will, of course. That attorney will probably charge them the statutory rate. In Florida, for example, there is an attorney fee rate schedule of what it costs to probate an estate in court. Depending on the size of the estate, an attorney can charge you a percentage of that fee. If you have $100,000 in total assets, you're probably looking at $3,000 in attorney's fees, plus probate costs. Probate will cost between $400 and $700, not to mention the expense of time that your family must spend to jump through all the hoops that the probate court requires.

Again, that free will cost your family $3,700 in the long-run, plus hours of time and frustration to work with the attorney and get through all the legal "mumbo jumbo."

The main thing you need to learn is that the "Penny-Pincher" planner in my example gave bad advice as a loss leader so that he or she could get more profitable legal work in the future. Not all free or inexpensive providers will use this scheme, but it is a very real problem, of which you should be aware. There can also be other problems associated with these types of providers, which is explained in chapters six, seven, and nine.

Other providers who charge a low price may not have a great deal of expertise in wills and trust planning because it is not their specialization. They know the basics in order to avoid malpractice and a lawsuit, but they may just be a general practitioner in that area of law, which I'll discuss further in chapter 9. They give you the basic advice and say, "Hey do these documents look good? Are the names spelled right?" and so forth, but their conversation with you stops there.

The worst part about persons who prepare cheap wills is that they can lead you to a false sense of security about your estate plan. It is very easy to think, "Why would I go to any other attorney? This one was nice, cheap, and everything looked fine."

However, that person and the resulting estate "plan" will only cover one layer of the onion: who gets what and who does what. One of the first things I learned in law school is that you need to peel back the layers of the onion. If you pull this string, what happens? If you pull that string, will one, two, or three happen? A good attorney who practices primarily in estate planning will think about how peeling back each layer will affect their client's future costs of time and money. They will take time and care to prevent future problems with a will, rather than seek future legal work or to add apparent value to his or her practice.

What If I Do Have a Tight Budget Right Now?

It is foolish for any healthy person with assets over $50,000 (including life insurance death proceeds) to choose a low cost provider. There are legal aid clinics in most geographic regions that can help if your assets or income are very low. Just make sure you get healthcare directives and a durable power of attorney with a long term care planning focus and language.

What's The Bottom Line?

Remember that the value of an attorney is in the advice they give you, not a signed piece of paper. You should now be able to spot a bad provider right off the bat. Their prices will usually be cheap (I usually see the budget provider prices under $300), but their forms are most likely filled in by other people out of a simple form book, and you will only review your documents and meet with the provider for a few minutes.

I recommend that you tread carefully and seek out an attorney who will spend more time with you, because a bad provider will cause more problems than they solve.

3. THE "PENNY-PINCHER" ESTATE PLAN

In the previous chapter, I discussed the problem with providers with poor processes who charged the rock bottom price, but what you got was a lousy will. Now I will further discuss a "Penny-Pincher," or low-budget, estate plan. The "I want just the documents" plan. The purpose of this chapter is to help you determine, wherever you go to get your estate planning done, whether you are getting ineffective legal planning. When I say, "ineffective," I mean planning that not actually happen how you want it to happen. You can also use this information to determine if you're getting ripped off with the final work product.

I often hear the question, "Why should I even hire an attorney when I can do it for free, or cheap and easy online by myself?" After reading chapter two, you might already be able to answer that question partially. To somebody like me, who practices estate planning law every day, full time, that question is the equivalent of a patient who asks their doctor, "Why do I need to pay you to perform this surgery when I can look on WebMD and Grey's

Anatomy to see how to do it?" Or, "I can just show my neighbor how to do it and he can do it for me. Why do I want to deal with insurance companies or doctors to perform the surgery?" Yikes!

Theoretically, if you have enough time to learn about wills, trust, probate, guardianship, Medicaid, tax, asset protection, social security, and advance directive law, then yes, you can know what information to input into online estate planning forms. You would also know what to add in addition to what the template forms do not contain. I do not want to sound obnoxious, but that is what it takes to complete free online, or cheap-and-easy will forms properly. The online wills simply discount the seven years of college and law school, and years of experience that a full-time estate planning attorney has. Experienced estate planning attorneys have advised people and properly structured their estates, not to mention have experienced correcting poorly drafted estate plans. They have had to sort out wills in probate court or other types of estate related administrative proceedings.

Will an Online Will Work For Me?

There are many options out there, and I'll first go through the cheap-and-easy online will and then the minefield of unlicensed practitioners of law. First, I want to tell you this book is about hiring a lawyer and paying for the right plan, and not about choosing a freebie or cheap program. In some cases, as I'll explain, online based programs might be a viable option and may satisfactorily get something in place for your will. There are some situations where having something is better than having nothing.

Certain online legal programs are halfway decent. I've seen a lot of them. The problem I've seen in the past is that online will programs lead you into a false sense of security about the effectiveness of their document. The keyword here is "document," which singular. The online program does not give advice that is relevant to your life situation and has a one-size-fits-all form.

Some online programs say that an attorney will review your estate plan, which is misleading. An attorney will spend very little time to review your plan and will just make sure your final product does not suffer from "user input error," and the probate court fight that will result. Will the attorney take time to get to know you and your personal situation? How much time do they give to help, teach, and counsel you about your options? An attorney behind the computer screen is similar to the attorney described in the previous chapter, who plugs in names on a generic form and only meets with you for a few minutes.

I've had people bring me online documents before and ask, "Do these documents look okay?" Well, I can never know that without knowing that person's family decision or family dynamics. Your legal documents must fit your personal situation. Second marriage third marriage, step-kids, half kids, illegitimate children born out of wedlock, kids with dependency issues, kids with special needs, affectionate relationships not in the family tree, and other family dynamics. That knowledge is learned only from a conversation, which is not part of an online legal program.

Financial gurus in the media such as Dave Ramsey and Susie Orman have advocated the need to create a simple will. Dave Ramsey's program promotes estate planning creation very early in the program. The problem with the estate planning advice by these financial gurus is that they are debt management gurus, and you may not be part of their target audience who would benefit from an online legal service or simple will.

Their intended audience are families who are working hard to focus on debt management and budgeting. These families might not be able to afford to hire an attorney just yet. What those financial experts advocate is for everyone to get at least some type of will in case of a catastrophic illness, accident, or death. At least something will be in place so your family can avoid a court-supervised guardianship or probate. If a family cannot afford to pay for an attorney, or currently does not have the income to justify the expense of paying a qualified estate planning attorney, then an online legal service advocated by Dave Ramsey or Susie Orman might be the right fit. It will help you get something in place until a later date when you are able to see an attorney for a more thorough estate plan. If you can afford to pay a qualified attorney at the current time, I highly recommend that you do so.

If you are in a situation where you must get a basic will, I also recommend trying to spend at least 30 minutes with an attorney to make sure that everything has a correct title. For example, a common problem is when term life insurance names your child under 18 as a contingent beneficiary (heir). In this case, a guardianship must be set up for the child to get all of the money when he or she turns 18. An estate planning attorney can set your life insurance up correctly as long as your will is done right too. Another example that can be even more problematic is if you are a divorced, single parent and you have named your child under 18 as the beneficiary of your life insurance. If you pass away, then the person in prime position to be the guardian over that money is your ex-spouse. You are almost making your ex-spouse your beneficiary of your estate. If you cannot afford to pay a qualified attorney at the current time, you can seek out a Legal Aid service in your area.

Should I Hire an Independent Paralegal?

Other than wills that you can pay for online, I have commonly seen estate plans advertised through independent paralegals, or document preparers who promote their services on websites like Craigslist, or on flyers and signs on the corners of busy intersections. The big problem with hiring a paralegal to write your will is that they are not working under the direction of an attorney. In some states, like Florida, this is illegal because they are an unlicensed practitioner of law. In my own experience with paralegals whom I have hired and trained (who have been wonderful and do great work), I can always spot mistakes they have made. This happens even under my direction using my established forms and guidelines. There's always a way in which my experience and education can be used to improve upon their work and get a better result for my clients. If one of my paralegals were to steal my forms, go off on their own, and advertise on the side of the road, she might do all right (if her business were legal). But again, her clients would not get education, background, and counseling advice along with those forms and the paralegal might not understand how to use the forms correctly in all circumstances or know how to adjust them correctly when needed.

You may have noticed that I stated the paralegals in my office use forms I have established. Estate planning attorneys will always use a base form, but the adjustments the attorney makes to the base form to tailor it to your situation is the value that you pay for when you hire an attorney.

Another noteworthy problem with using a paralegal service is that paralegals do not have the roots in the community to stand by their work if something goes wrong. They do not have the same followthrough, responsibility, or liability that an attorney has, which is another part of the value when you hire an attorney versus a paralegal to prepare your estate plan. An attorney who takes your money and doesn't do the work risks disbarment and loss of their license that he or she spend seven years of education to get. A paralegal may risk criminal charges for unauthorized practice of law, but they do not have a license that they risk losing. Although many paralegals do get formal training, anyone can call themselves a paralegal without any formal training at all.

Should I Get a Revocable Living Trust?

Another type of an estate plan I have seen advertised is a revocable living trust. These are often advertised as seminars and are put on by financial planners. A revocable living trust is a type of estate planning document that is similar to a will, but is specifically set up to avoid probate. Most of the time, I see that these are set up by insurance companies. The insurance companies will put their agents (who require no college education) out in the field to do canned presentations about revocable living trust plans and how to avoid probate. Once again, you run into the same one-size-fits-all form that has been a recurring theme throughout this book. The insurance agents will always try to say, "We have an attorney," but a lot of times the attorney just plugs names into documents, and they do not appropriately consider the family situation. The big problem there is that since the insurance agent does all of the consulting, and you do not meet face to face with an attorney, the insurance agent is illegally practicing law, according to some states like Florida. It is not an attorney with experience who learns about your personal situation.

Another problem with revocable living trust seminars is that insurance agents primarily use their presentations to lure people in and sell high-commission insurance products. Depending on how much money you put into these insurance products, their commission can far exceed what any normal estate planning attorney will charge.

Can I Just Do It Myself?

The last form of estate planning that I have seen and will discuss is the "do it yourself" version, which comes with a huge warning. It is possible to go to legal libraries, look in their form books, and find examples of wills. You can type them out yourself, and plug in some names. Even worse, you can get forms at an ordinary office supply store. That is venturing into the same realm as using Web MD to diagnose and treat your own illnesses. You don't know what you don't know. If you are inclined to do it yourself then know this, a lot of good attorneys will not do their own estate planning documents because they know about the pitfalls involved. I personally will not handle certain matters of my own, such as buying a house. Although I have done real estate closings for clients, I wouldn't want to do my own real estate closing because it is difficult to see things objectively. When you handle your own legal work, you often see things how you want to see them, which might not be consistent with reality or the law. Because of the importance of your family, it always pays to have an independent or third party look at things for you so they can see things that you don't know and that you don't see.

Some Final Thoughts

What I'd like for you to take away from this chapter is that "Penny-Pincher" estate plans can work to get something down to direct how you would like your affairs to be handled for your incapacity and death planning, but an incomplete document that doesn't meet your needs could lead to problems for you and your family down the road because you don't know what you don't know!

4. THE PERFECT PLANNING TRIANGLE

In this chapter, you will learn what needs to happen in order for your estate planning be effective. If these underlying issues are not developed properly before you see your final estate planning documents, then you should question whether or not you have an effective plan in place.

In order to have a great estate plan, it should be set up as a perfect planning triangle. The perfect planning triangle has three sides.

First, personal family situation.

Second, plans and goals.

Third, legal implementation of your plan.

These three sides must all work together. When there is a change of facts on one side of the triangle, the other two sides of can be affected, which can cause costly problems down the road for your family if ignored.

I've created a special report that details the perfect planning triangle, but in this chapter I will review the concept with you in abbreviated fashion. If you want more information on the report, you can certainly contact me and request it.

Your Personal Family Situation

The first part of the perfect planning triangle involves your personal family situation. Many people think their family is mundane. "I have a wife. I have two kids. I'm just like everyone else." In reality though, families are very different from household to household. When you say you are like everyone else, "everyone else" means everyone you know closely or who lives around you. The people I know on a close, personal level seem just like me as well. But the people who you are close to are probably much different from the people who I am close to.

An attorney must weigh and discuss your family and how they are related to each other. Some families might have a child who is not responsible with money, or a child with a spendthrift spouse who is untrustworthy. You might have children from a previous relationship. Your personal family situation does not only include your spouse, children, and grandchildren, but can also include your parents, siblings, caregivers, neighbors, estranged children, or other people regularly involved in your life. In order to have an estate plan, your personal family situation needs to be flushed out, discussed, and carefully considered with your attorney.

Your personal family situation is also affected by your personal financial situation. This includes types of assets you own, liabilities, income sources, and other financial information that has a role in your personal family situation. You might also think everybody has a retirement plan, money in the bank, and maybe a house. Well, this is not always the case, and it turns out that a lot of people can have other obscure assets, some of which are mentioned in chapter one. Rental properties, tractor trailers, oil well interests, and other things that are not readily apparent will require special consideration from an attorney.

Another part of your financial situation is the current titling of your assets. The title on the assets is the name on the account. You might receive a bank statement with just your name only, which means the account is titled "individually," not in conjunction with other family members. A great deal of estate planning involves whose names are on each account and how each account is set up.

Your so-called net worth will probably vary greatly from other individuals. Many people think estate planning is something that you do if you have millions of dollars, but this is not necessarily true. A positive net worth is a positive net worth, and you do have money. In reality, if you have $60,000 at 85 years old you still have money, and you need to at least have healthcare planning documents in order to avoid probate and guardianship problems. The more money you have, the more likely you need to plan your estate carefully because a larger estate means more money to fight over and the more money available to pay for attorneys to fight each other.

The next financial variable is your income, and how your family situation influences your income. Many questions can come into play. Are there opportunities to receive more income that is available to you? What happens to a pension of one spouse if he or she dies first? An estate planning attorney can help refer you to financial professionals who work closely with the attorney to solve any income problems, in addition to income advice that relates to public benefits, such as social security, Medicare, and Medicaid programs.

One last piece that ties into your personal family situation is your personal physical situation. I've worked with young families who have their first baby, and families who are older and in their 90's. Health situations vary due to age and can effect the family aspect of your estate plan. The family members who you take care of, and the family members who take care of you will change throughout your lifetime.

Your Goals and Plans

The second part of the perfect estate planning triangle is your goals and plans for you, your estate, and your family. An estate planning attorney teaches you important issues to think about and plan for. Here are some key questions to consider when deciding your goals and plans:

- What do you want to do with your money today?
- What did you want to do with your money when you first set

up your estate?

- If you have an existing set of documents, why did you have them created for you and what do you want to change?

- What do you want to happen to your money when you pass away?

- What message do you want to make clear about your money if you're disabled?

- Is your money going to be focused on you, your care, and needs? Would you like to plan your child's inheritance?

- What is the rationale behind your plans?

- Are you concerned about someone in your family receiving a large amount of money?

- Do you think someone in your family would challenge your estate?

- Do you want court intervention or supervision?

- Do you want government supervision?

- Do you want to prevent all your money going to a nursing home?

- Do you want to prevent your surviving spouse from disinheriting your children?

- Do you want to keep your estate out of the hands of your in-laws?

- Do you want to reduce taxes?

The list of questions can go on, and each requires thoughtful planning.

Legal Implementation of Your Plan

The last part of the triangle is the legal implementation of your estate plan. After understanding your personal family situation, financial situation, current health, along with your goals and plans, the estate planning attorney's task is to put your goals, plans and directions on paper clearly. Everything must be committed to a comprehensive legal document.

In summary, when you begin the estate planning process you must first seek education about different options in your estate plan. The attorney should be able to counsel you about tough choices and tell you what options you have. Then, you and your attorney can decide what to do about those tough choices and make decisions with which you are comfortable. Once you settle the plans, you and your attorney will decide how to implement them. Legal documents will be put in place that are structured and worded correctly to implement the plans at the proper time.

Let's put it all together... The right estate planning attorney's legal implementation will properly translate your personal situation with your goals and plans, so the outcome is just how you would like it. Your family will not refer to handling your affairs as "a nightmare." You should look for an estate planning attorney who does all of these things.

5. THE PLANNING PROCESS

Education-Based Planning Process

In the previous chapter, I mention the type of estate plan and process that a good attorney will use. Once you find your attorney you should ask about their process, and the experience that you will go through as a client to get the results that you want. This chapter is here to help guide you through process you should expect from an attorney who will create your estate plan.

First, you've got to make sure that the process the attorney uses is an educational and consultation based process versus a mechanical, or fill-in-the-blank process. An educational-based attorney will cost more because you will get to spend more time with that attorney, learning about the various legal issues necessary in estate planning. They will be well worth the extra cost. An educational-based attorney should also have multiple handouts, reports and seminar materials, videos and so forth to help you better understand your legal issue and what to consider before your consultation.

Remember, not everyone's legal needs are the same, so the better handle you have on your specific legal issues, the better questions you can ask during your personal one-on-one time with an attorney. The educational materials that your attorney provides for you should help you learn everything you need to know to work with him or her effectively. Hopefully, you will be able to grasp the core estate issues so well that you are able to spot many of your own needs, bring up relevant information in your meeting, and ask your attorney challenging questions that may even require him or her to do extra research. As you learned in the previous chapter, everyone's personal situations are very different and complex. The better educated you are, the better position you will be in to know what elements of your background are most important to share.

Say, for example, you are a male who had a child out of wedlock. You may read through the materials that your attorney provided you and learn that the child can make a claim against your estate when you die. When it's time for your consultation with your attorney, he or she will ask you about potential heirs of your estate, and you will know to bring up the important information about that child. The attorney can then effectively handle that issue so an estate challenge does not pop up in the future. That is a good outcome for someone who works with an attorney who uses an educational-based process.

The educational process is not meant to confuse or overwhelm you with information, but should prepare for an efficient meeting with your attorney. If you have no knowledge of estate planning when you meet with your attorney, he or she must spend extra time to explain information, or probe you for more details about your personal family and financial situations. Your attorney will most likely bill you for the extra hours that he or she spends with you, so if you educate yourself ahead of time, you can save time and money.

Mechanical-Based Planning Process

Let's compare and education-based process to a mechanical-based process, which is usually a strong element of estate planning "mills". A mechanical planner just asks you direct questions that you answer. Usually, no background information is asked, nor is there conversation about why the questions are relevant and important to you. Then, your answers end up in template form. The mechanical process is, of course, less expensive, but it is just document production and fill-in-the-blank work. As you can see, the educational-based, consultation based practice goes much deeper. This process involves counseling to learn about your total legal situation, your personal situation, your financial situation, and your family situation.

Steps in the Educational and Consultation-Based Process

When you work with an estate planning attorney, you will see some division of labor between positions at an estate planning firm. You shouldn't be worried if other employees at the firm are doing certain elements of your work. The attorney's job is to learn your personal situation and guide you to the planning result that you want and then direct his team to implement his plan with certain drafting techniques and properly setting up an account. One pitfall that you may want to look out for is an attorney who does too much of the work himself or herself, and charges you for the work that could be done by a paralegal or associate attorney. You want your attorney to be involved with you, but you should know that some division of labor is necessary to achieve the best result for your estate plan and to keep costs lower.

With that said, here is a typical rundown of an estate planning process. The first thing that will happen when you call the office is to receive educational and informational materials, so you can better educate yourself on what needs to go into your estate plan. Some attorneys will provide written materials, an educational seminar or workshop that you may attend, or both. You may be encouraged to schedule an appointment at this time, but if you are not ready to work with an attorney yet, the appointment can be scheduled when you are ready.

After you receive the information, you should study it and attend the seminar to educate yourself on the planning process.

Then, you will likely meet with somebody, an attorney or paralegal, for your first meeting. At this first meeting, the purpose is to develop and understand your primary planning goals and get a handle on the nature of your family and your assets.

After the attorney or paralegal has a clear understanding of your situation, they will inform you about your planning options and the cost of implementation. Given the level of complexity of your planning, your planning can be drafted at that meeting, or the design of your plan can be established at that meeting. If you have a more complicated solution or more complicated needs, there will be another meeting scheduled.

If you have a less-complicated estate, the estate planning attorney or firm will draft your estate plan documents in between your first and second meeting. The second meeting is designed to review your estate plan documents and to execute or sign them. In more complicated estate plans, the second meeting will be used to further hammer down your planning decisions and get down to more of the specifics. Typically, depending on the level of complication, whether you have a business tax or elder care planning need, you may even need additional meetings and planning sessions to get to your final result.

Once you and your attorney hash out your estate plan, then he or she will prepare the estate planning instruments. On your final meeting, you will get to review the documents. Some attorneys will provide drafts in advance, some will not. It is more efficient for you to review the drafts with the attorney explaining each instrument to you. You'll have time to make changes, ask questions about the legal effect of certain written provisions, and then ultimately sign the documents.

Last, if you need to fund any trusts in your estate plan, you must know whether or not the estate planning firm will put the assets in the trust for you, or whether someone else will handle this process. Your attorney may advise you on how to do it yourself, or you may have the option to hire an outside source to do the additional work. You should discuss this step with your attorney in your initial meetings, so you know what to expect. Chapter ten includes more information about the topic.

When Should I Update My Estate Plan?

Some attorney's offices offer ongoing maintenance programs for an annual or monthly fee. Some attorney's offices will charge you a fee as the updates need to be made. Typically, you will need to update your estate planning documents due to one of four primary changes. First, a *change in people*. Change in people occurs when the people who you've named in your estate planning documents have changed. Maybe someone has passed away, someone is born, someone is married or divorced, someone has formed an addiction, someone was in an unfortunate accident, and so forth.

The second reason to update or make an adjustment to your

estate plan is if you have a *change in money*. Your documents may provide gifts of certain assets that are no longer in your estate because you have sold them or given them away, or you may have received an inheritance or other kind of windfall, which has changed the money that you have in your estate. Those are just a couple of examples.

The third reason to update is because of a *change in your goals*. Your existing estate plan may have certain provisions because of the time in your life that you set them up. Over time, those goals may change. Let me explain. When you are a young parent and have minors under 18, your will should be set up in a certain way to provide for your children in case something was to happen to you before they turn 18. Your estate plan will delegate what happens to the money and who manages it. Thirty years later, when your kids are 40, that old will does not meet your goals, and you may want to revisit them and adjust accordingly.

The last reason is when there is a *change in the law*. Changes in the law will sometimes have a retroactive effect, meaning that if your estate planning documents were signed prior to a certain date, then you are grandfathered in and won't need to make a change. Some estate planning laws have immediate effect. The best way to stay updated is to make sure that the attorney you're working with has a process to advise his or her clients about estate planning updates and changes in the law.

6. CAN THE TV AND BILLBOARD ATTORNEY HELP?

At this point, I hope you have realized that planning your estate is not simply plugging in names into blank lines in the same documents, over and over again, without any consideration other than spelling of names. If you still believe estate planning is a simple fill in the blank exercise, then you should probably stop reading. If you want to make sure that you do it right and define the result for your family, the next few chapters will help you narrow down who to hire.

Can TV and billboard attorneys help? The most common attorneys who you see on TV and billboards are usually part of a personal injury law practice. Yes, they can help you with your will, but you should not be blinded by their celebrity and forget to look out for the same big issues that I explained in previous chapters.

You should beware of: (1) use of your will as a loss leader; (2) non-specialization[2] or focus; (3) lack of consultation and education. The main issue is that a lot of attorneys who mass advertise may think that estate planning is as simple as you might have thought before you started reading the first couple chapters in this book. Those attorneys might have forms that a first year attorney or law student prepared and they simply plug in the names. Of course, this may not be the case for all billboard attorneys, but you should proceed with caution and pay attention to the process that they use, as outlined in chapters 4 and 5.

You should be careful to make sure that your will is not used as a loss leader for the attorney. You do not want your attorney to do your estate plan in order to get a personal injury case from youlater, in which they have a chance to make hundreds of thousands of dollars. In fact, a major goal of your estate plan is to avoid legal issues in the future. When choosing to work with any attorney, make sure they will take the time to educate and counsel you to get the right plan in place for you and your family. You do not want to hire any attorney who takes just any case in order to cover their high costs of advertising.

You must also be careful about the frequency of which the

---

[2] Legal ethics rules prohibit the term "specialist," "specialty," or "expert" as it relates to an attorney's law practice. I'm not referring to myself, or others, as specialists. When I use these terms in this book, they are a short-hand term for "an attorney whose sole function in law practice is to help people plan their estate."

attorney practices in your area of need. This rule of thumb will apply for any legal issue. For example, if you have a social security disability issue, you want an attorney who (1) commits a vast majority of their practice to issues that surround social security disability, (2) speaks to you directly about case strategy, and not only through support staff, and (3) does not simply "fill in the blanks." In another example, if you need a commercial lease, you should find an attorney who deals with commercial real estate, and if you can find one who does a lot of commercial leasing, that's probably your guy!

The attorney who regularly advertises another area of law, such as personal injury, probably does not focus his or her practice in estate planning law. They have probably developed their skills and abilities perfectly to fit their main area of law practice. Attorney practices require different skills and strengths for each legal issue. A trial lawyer in a personal injury case may need to be a "shark" because he or she has to win a court case for their client, which could be exactly what their client needs. On the other hand, an estate planning attorney may need to have a teach personality to teach and consult their clients about the legal issues that confront them.

An estate planning attorney is an attorney who must know and explain the legal effect that your death and incapacity have on your financial affairs. The estate planning attorney helps you maintain as much control as you desire, from when you are in perfect health to 50 years after you pass away. Your banker, even though he or she gives you legal advice when telling you how to name your account, is not an estate planning attorney. The estate planning attorney marries will, trust, probate, guardianship, tax, Medicaid, veteran's benefits, social security, IRA, and many other similar areas of law, to create the best outcome for you and your family upon your death, or incapacitation.

7. "HOW DO I FIGURE OUT WHO I'M EVEN LOOKING FOR?"

In the last chapter I defined who an estate planning attorney is, along with a caution about the TV or billboard attorney who might not be your best fit for estate planning law. In this chapter, I'm going to talk about general practice attorneys and some problems associated with them, along with some of the problems associated with, what I call, "old school" attorneys. You will find "Penny-Pincher" attorneys included in this group. Then, I will discuss the "trust mill" attorney. Last, I will introduce you to the types of estate planning attorney sub-specialists who focus on very specific issues.

General Practice Attorneys

General practice attorneys deal with a broad range of legal areas. A problem with this is that he or she may lack expertise or specific, special knowledge in any one area of law. They generally lack the depth of knowledge and expertise that an estate planning attorney has. As you learned in the previous chapter, the estate planning attorney must understand several different areas just to be a good estate planning attorney. Their "well" of knowledge must be narrow and deep. The general practice attorney might practice all of the estate planning areas of law, plus they may also do criminal, family law, personal injury, or social security law, which have no cross-over to estate planning law. The general practice attorney's "well" of knowledge is shallow and wide.

The general practice attorney might consult with you about your will in the morning, but then around lunch they may meet with another client about a divorce. After lunch, they may be off to a court hearing relating to a criminal case, and at 4:00 PM they may attend a real estate closing.

That attorney is not committing malpractice, or doing anything illegal. That is just how his or her practice is set up. This approach may be just fine for some people who have small families and lower amount of assets. He or she performs competently, but does not get too deep in the well. He or she does not peel many layers of the onion, so to speak. He may attack your core legal issue that must be handled right away, but not always consider the other issues that could thwart your ultimate goals down the road.

General Estate Practice Attorneys

A general estate practice attorney is a little more focused in their law practice. General estate practice deals with wills, trusts, estates, durable power of attorney, healthcare surrogates, living will, probate, guardianship, and so forth. The issue with a general estate practice is that you sometimes can run into the "mill" practice. That means that everyone who comes in the door gets the "X" plan with no variations.

The general estate or "mill" practice is most common in the advertisement and promotion of revocable living trusts. Revocable living trusts can be great, and they can get great results for families, but there is another level of education of you required, because a trust is not immediately intuitive. Most law schools devote a couple months to this concept, so it is not something that the average citizen would normally have knowledge about. A trust mill can sometimes be one of those situations where you give an attorney a list of your family's names, and they only review the documents with you for a small amount of time. The attorney does this in order to meet their profit goal. Some families come out of their planning meeting with plans that are not completely followed through on because the general estates practice may not be able to give full instructions to the client. For example, when you create a trust, there is a second step that is required to make the trust actually work. This is called "funding the trust." This step is often missed.

The general estate practice will usually charge lower prices than a specialist, but in order to justify those lower prices, they might rely on paralegals to do a lot of the legwork, such as asking you "who gets what" and "who does what". The paralegal would then plug in blanks on the form and then you will review it with the attorney. This does save you a lot of money, but you may not realize the things that are missing, or what you family would actually have to go through when you pass. Candidly, there is legwork that is easier for you to accomplish and cheaper for you to accomplish than if you were to go through the attorney's office. However, if you want to make sure it's done right and not having to require so much legwork from you, then that's something you're going to end up paying more money for in the ultimate price of your estate plan and the total cost that you're going to pay to set it up.

Attorneys With a Sub-Specialty

The first area of sub-specialty is a **business estate planning attorney**. In chapter one, I mentioned that you can do estate planning for your business. A business estate planning attorney will have the greatest deal of knowledge and background for any large or small business. They understand estate planning principles, general business principles, business finance, business management structure, and business structure principles, like corporation and LLC set up. They will make sure the language in the governing documents for your business correlates with an estate planning set of documents. He or she will know how to set up succession planning and asset protection related to your business. They can tell you how to set up your business so that your business partners (or specific family members) would be able to buy out your share in the business if you were to pass away. Those are the kinds of issues a business estate planning attorney can help you with.

The next area of sub-specialty for estate planning is **asset protection planning**. Asset protection planning can apply to a couple types of practice areas, but most commonly means asset protection in the here and now. If you are in a high liability business or profession, and you are worried about a lawsuit now or in the future, then an asset protection estate planning attorney can help you. They can protect your assets and make sure liabilities are reduced for lawsuits. That type of estate planning attorney must know rules about fraudulent transfers, which have to do with a transfer of money that might defray or defraud a creditor of you right now. For example, if you are sued, it would be fraudulent for you to give away all your money to your mother in order to avoid the judgment that you are facing. If you do that, the person to whom you owe money can actually sue your mom to get that money back as if it were in your possession. The asset protection attorney could counsel you to avoid serious legal mistakes and help you protect your money in other ways. An asset protection attorney will also have knowledge that relates to bankruptcy, special types of trusts, titling of assets, and provisions in Florida law that allow you to protect your assets from creditors.

A third type of sub-specialty estate planning attorney is **elder law**. Elder law focuses on capacity issues of an elderly person and what happens if they become incapacitated. An elder law attorney can help protect and preserve assets from assisted living and nursing home facilities. They work with families who have a loved one with dementia, a recent dementia diagnosis, or who have a family history of dementia. They work with families who have concerns about the rising cost of long term care and going broke, or losing all of their money to a nursing home. Elder law attorneys work with folks worried about long term care costs or costs associated with other things that happen to you before you die.

A fourth type of sub-specialty estate planning attorney is the **estate tax planning attorney**. Estate tax is a form of taxation that occurs after you have already paid income tax on your money. An inheritance is an example of an estate tax that can be found at the federal and the state level. Federal estate taxes can apply to families with at least $5 million in total assets, including life insurance money. This number changes every single year and, in fact, it's a little higher than $5 million at the time of this publication. ($5 million is a basic guide point.) If you have over a $1 million in assets, you should always keep your ears open to what congress does in relation to the gift, trust, estate, and inheritance tax regime because that changes every year. It is best to have an attorney who consistently deals with estate tax reduction and legal avoidance techniques to assist you with your needs.

The last and fifth most common estate planning sub-specialty is **special needs planning**. If you have a young child, or adult child who has a developmental disability, or requires special care, then a special needs planning attorney can set up your estate and also structure their affairs. A special needs planning attorney would make sure that any government assistance they receive, such as group home funding or caregiver assistance, will not be disrupted if they receive an inheritance from you.

How Do I Choose the Right Type of Attorney?

You can further determine the difference between attorneys and their sub-specialties when doing some research on the local attorneys in your area. The best place to start is usually through the Internet or yellow pages. When searching the Internet, you need to think about the core legal issue which prompted you to request this book your are currently reading. Think about what drove your interest in estate planning. For example, it could be, "How do I plan for my kids under the age of 14 if something were to happen to me?" You can type that exact question into a Google search box, and you will be sure to get a couple of good suggestions and good information on where to start and drive your search further. While you're at it, go ahead and turn to the work page in the very back of this book and write down your "Core

Legal Issue" at the top. This will help you stay focused on your goal throughout your entire search process.

Once you have a handle on your core legal concern, you are then able to look for attorneys in your area who can provide services that echo the research, terms, and the information that you found.

Now you've seen the differences between the types of attorneys who are out there. Consider what you need. If you are thinking about the general practice attorney, then you will probably pay a little bit lower price than an attorney that has a sub-specialty. If you would like to get help from an estate planning attorney with a sub-specialty, then you will pay higher fees, but you will have a higher level of sophistication in your estate plan. In the next chapter, you will learn how to locate these attorneys in your own independent research.

8. HOW TO NARROW DOWN YOUR SEARCH

The first thing that you're going to need to do is choose from the sub-specialties and discover your core, most important legal issue that drives your need for estate planning. Part of doing your research will involve educating yourself about different estate planning topics within each attorney sub-specialty. You learned about this in the previous chapter. There are two main ways to begin to narrow your list down to two or three attorneys. The first way is through advertising, and the second way is through word of mouth. As you continue to narrow down your search, remember to complete the work page in the back of the book to organize your thoughts and information about the attorneys in your area.

Narrowing Down A Search Through Attorney Advertising

The two most common ways to find an estate planning attorney through advertising are the Internet and the yellow pages.

If you start with the yellow pages, you might look for a "Will/Trusts" lawyer heading, or "Estate Planning," or "Elder Law." I think it is extremely helpful to cross-reference your search using the Internet. Look at each attorney's website and view the information they provide. If you are not an Internet user, then I recommend that you call up each attorney's office on the yellow pages listing and ask the questions that I will review in detail in the forthcoming chapters. At this point, you should not ask for prices or to set up an appointment. What you should seek is *additional information* that can be sent to you after you make the calls, such as a brochure, a live seminar, report, book, audio recording, or video. The attorney should have this type of information available. If not, then that attorney will more than likely be a budget, or mechanical attorney.

You can also find estate planning attorneys through general Internet searches, by searching "estate planning attorneys" in your specific city. You can look in online directories for estate planning attorneys, but ultimately, you want to end up on the attorney's website so you can evaluate his business practices and additional estate planning information. An attorney or law firm's website should hopefully be an enhanced, interactive brochure for you to gather the information you need.

In your Internet research, you will probably not find many large law firms. Surprisingly, they have not caught up to smaller law firms in terms of Internet presence because of the red tape that each attorney in the firm must go through in order for their advertising to be approved. On the Internet, you will most likely be able to research estate planning attorneys in small or medium-sized law firms, including sole practitioners.

When you look at the websites attorneys, most of the time you'll determine that the websites are very similar. In particular, you'll see a profile of the attorney, the kinds of practice areas they have, and so forth. One of the most important things to look out for is this: **Is this attorney a sole practitioner who is advertising his or her services for estate planning, among several other areas of law?**

Again, just like the previous chapter when I talked about general attorneys, you may want to stray from attorneys who do not have synergistic, related correlations between the areas of law they practice. For example, criminal law is not closely related to wills and trusts. An attorney who practices both will not handle estate planning at the level of somebody who solely practices estate planning law.

Family law attorneys most commonly dabble in estate planning, and depending on your situation, the family law attorney may or may not have the necessary tools to plan correctly for you. You may also have headaches trying to finalize your estate planning with a family law attorney who is always in court. On the other hand, if you have recently divorced, or may remarry when you have kids, then a family law attorney who has some strong estate planning background may be useful. Believe it or not, the use of prenuptial agreements and postnuptial agreements are quite common in estate planning, and the prenup is not just for divorces and settlement. Once again, it's important for you to keep your core legal issue in mind when researching attorneys to find what you need.

Getting back to the phone book: you have to watch the listings to make sure you call someone who focuses solely in estate planning, and not a bunch of other legal practice areas. The big issue with the yellow pages is that you will indeed find attorneys who pay a lot of money to advertise in the yellow pages and they get to place their ad in additional practice areas, which is thrown in as part of their yellow pages deal. You will find some attorneys who do not solely focus in estate planning law, but they practice personal injury law. They spend so much money with the yellow pages that they are able to get additional listings and practice areas where they're not sharply focused.

Online Directories

Online directories are similar to the phone book. Some of the most common directories are attorney ratings websites. Some of these ratings can be accurate; some may be inaccurate. I am aware of attorneys who have poor reputations among the legal community, who do not produce good results or have little experience, yet are able to "work" some of the rating systems to get a higher rating. This is obviously deceptive to their potential clients. Attorneys can manipulate some (not all) rating sites by asking all of their friends and colleagues to endorse them, which helps to increase their rating or helps to get on certain other lists. Rating systems are good tools, but they should not be the ultimate end all, be all in your search. They are a good cross-referencing tool as you look for consistency in your research.

Other Advertising Media

Now on to the lesser used advertising media. You will also see attorneys advertising on T.V., radio and billboards. Most recently, I've seen billboards with general practice attorneys advertising estate planning. It is very rare in my area to see an estate planning attorney using T.V., radio or billboard advertising. If the attorney is offering free information, then take it. It could be the start of your planning. You need to go further by cross-referencing word of mouth and what you can find on the Internet about that attorney.

Newspapers and direct mail are very common ways of advertising for estate planning attorneys because the estate planning process should always start with an educational or reading component in order to educate you about your planning options. These educational print advertisements could do a better job to help you make the decisions to plan your estate.

Cross-References

After you've built up an awareness about different attorneys, you should certainly supplement your independent search with cross-referencing. Ask your family, friends, other attorneys, and money related professionals who you've worked with in the past if they can recommend an attorney for you to use. You need to continue to use the principles you learn in this book to vet out an attorney recommended to you – the attorney recommended by your friend might not be good, but your friend would be none the wiser because he or she hasn't read this book!

What Questions Should I Ask When Someone Refers an Attorney to Me?

First of all, make sure this person has actually worked with the attorney on estate planning, not another legal issue. Ask your friend about the process and time spent with that attorney. When an estate planning attorney works with somebody, if he is worth his salt, then he or she will end up spending more than at least three hours with that person. In order to do correct estate planning, the attorney needs to know about personal family information and financial situation as part of the perfect estate planning triangle. The process should not be like a doctor's appointment where you may speak with a doctor for 10 minutes, and then he's gone.

Next, ask others for their thoughts on the attorney's integrity.

Does that attorney do what they say, and say what they do? Will that attorney give advice and layout options, good and bad, for you? Does that attorney make recommendations that seem to further his or her financial interests rather than the client's estate plans?

Third, you must look out for the attorney's personality to determine if the attorney's personality will mix with you. As silly as it may sound, you may be "married" to that attorney for a while, and you want to make sure that you like the attorney as a person and professional. Some attorneys can vastly differ from other attorneys. For example, some attorneys are pretty dry, serious authority figures. Compare that to someone like me who is gregarious, but may get off-topic when conversing about personal interests. One is not better than the other, but the estate planning experience will be miserable if your personalities do not work well together.

Attorney personality is all about your personal preference. Some attorneys in the estate planning realm are not exactly aggressive and competitive, while most attorneys out there are. Since estate planning is not an adversarial or antagonistic practice of law, there are some estate planning attorneys who are a little reserved, a little calmer, than you might expect an attorney to be. This may help you feel more comfortable. Different personalities can sometimes lead people to think that a very competent attorney is not competent. If you have a particular concern about an attorney because of this, you can certainly ask the person referring you to them about it.

Fourth, you want to ask the person who's referring an attorney to you about *how thorough* that attorney is in their process of developing an estate plan with their clients. You should consult with somebody who is aware of that attorney and their practice to determine if that attorney's process is thorough enough that they will cover all bases in the planning process.

Last, you should ask your friend, or referral source, about price. Do not feel as though price is the main driver on how to choose the right attorney. You need to understand that most estate planning attorneys will charge differently based on different circumstances. You should be worried if the attorney charges the same price for all situations because this attorney probably is not giving out specific advice or planning. That attorney might be a generalist, and they may miss issues that are important to good planning. Further, your friend or family member might have different estate planning goals than you. If you are in the mindset, or the type of personality who wants the best, and your friend does not want the best of something you guys might have a disconnect. For example, if you are a Lexus driver and you ask a Toyota driver about cars and pricing, you will probably have different opinions about what a "good" car is.

Initially, you should take pricing with a grain of salt and to get an idea of what is typical so that you do not get ripped off. You can also check to see whether you could get underserved because of an exceedingly low price. An exceedingly low price would indicate that you will get a basic setup, or basic will, which might not take into consideration your particular needs.

To recap, you should inquire about the following pieces of information when an attorney is referred to you:

1. **Tested or played out experience by the person giving the referral**
2. **Integrity of the attorney**
3. **Personality of the attorney**
4. **Thoroughness of the attorney's process**
5. **Price, if you have similar issue as the person you are asking**

Who Can I Ask to Recommend an Estate Planning Attorney?

As already explained above, you could ask your friends. An important note is to ask friends who have similar issues or life situations. If you're in a group for moms who have toddlers or young kids, this is a topic for conversation that you could bring up. "Hey, did anyone set up a will or trust for their kids?" Then you can proceed to ask about the questions listed above. Your peers are a great source to help you get started.

Who you ask depends on where you are in life's journey. You may not get the best referral when you and a friend or family member are in different life stages. If you asked your kids whom they used, their attorney might not be as equipped to handle your estate. When the generations are different, there can be different issues in play. Consider asking your friends at church, or in a knitting group who are all near your same age and have similar family situations. Then the referral and the recommendation is going to be more accurate towards your needs.

Another great person to ask for a referral is **another attorney** who you know. Generally, attorneys are involved in professional associations and they will meet, interact, and work with other attorneys, even if they don't practice the same area of law. Attorneys can be a pretty good judge of character among their peers. They could be a good source to see if your research is correct about the estate planning attorneys you've looked at and previously researched.

The one downside to asking other attorneys is that you may get yourself in an uncomfortable position of the attorney saying "I can do that," when after reading this book, you feel that they're not the specialist that you need. So, that could be a downside.

Another downside might be to ask an attorney for a referral who works in a larger firm. If there's an estate planning attorney in their law firm, that means they will get increased compensation for referring you to that attorney. They get the money that stays "in-house" when the attorney in the law firm may not be, again, the best attorney for your specific legal need. The same can also be true for a smaller firm attorney. They can get a referral fee from the estate planning attorney to whom they refer a client. You can always ask follow-up questions like, "have you seen his work?" and "what is his reputation among clients whom you have previously referred that attorney?"

Next, you can ask other professionals who may advise you about your finances, such as **certified financial planners** (CFP®), certified public accountants, or life insurance professionals. Also, bank managers might know estate planning attorneys. Each of these financial professionals will have a varying level of experience with estate planning attorneys so their referrals and information may vary.

First, if you're working with a financial planner to help plan for your retirement and manage your investments, that profession is the most likely to refer you to an estate planning attorney who they have seen in action, which is crucial. Your financial planner is the best person to ask. Part of being a competent, qualified, and trusted certified financial planner is to make sure your clients have effective estate planning because estate planning is an essential component of the total financial and retirement plan.

Estate planning protects against legal loss from your estate. So, the certified financial planner is certainly in a great position to refer you to an attorney and describe the attorney's process, tell you what the attorney is like, and give you a general idea of pricing and where that attorney's prices fall in the spectrum of reasonability given the work product. They will also know how to catch too-expensive or too-cheap outliers in pricing.

One of the important things about pricing that you want to

watch out for are the outliers. Attorneys who charge too little may give deficient advice. Good attorneys who charge too much, recommend too much "legal medicine," so to speak. Watch out for being charged for an estate plan that is overly complex for your personal needs. Alternatively, the higher price might be the result of having the best reputation for good work in town. In that case, you will pay for the best. That attorney can charge as much as they want because they are the best (too high in demand, so they charge accordingly). You've got to decide whether or not you feel like you want to pay that.

Certified financial planners should also help guide you on what you can do with your estate plan, based on their experience working with attorneys who settle estates. They should know basic concepts and basic "hot button" issues that you need to plan for. That makes them a great referral source or cross-reference source because they will know what attorney is best to attack various issues.

The second type of financial professional that you may ask for a referral is an **accountant**. Because accountants work with money, they will typically need to refer clients to estate planning attorneys from time to time. Many accountants should know about quality estate tax estate planning attorneys and business estate planning attorneys. Accountants will run into the attorneys many times through continuing educations requirements, such as seminars and workshops. (The same goes for certified financial planners.) Accountants are not typically "out and about" as much as certified financial planners, so they might not have a long list of referrals or a stable knowledge base about the planning process. Typically, once an accountant trusts an attorney, that accountant may not deviate from referring only one or two names to their clients. They will always want feedback from their clients to make sure the estate planning attorney meets their needs. This makes them a good source in cross-referencing.

A third group of professionals to ask for a referral are **life insurance salespeople** and **annuity salespeople**. Some of these folks are very good, but a lot of them only know how estate planning relates to the sale their financial products. They are also very transaction-based versus relationship-based. If you purchase a financial product, such as a life insurance policy, your relationship might not be ongoing like a relationship with a certified financial planner or accountant. The life insurance professionals will know attorneys in town, and if they have been around long enough, they should know about estate planning attorneys and can be decent sources of cross-referencing.

The last good source to cross-reference and search for an estate planning attorney is through **aging-care providers**, such as geriatric care managers, social workers, hospital discharge planners, admission staff at nursing homes or assisted living facilities, and administrators of in-home care companies. These folks will typically work with estate planning attorneys who focus in elder law because they need to make sure that their clients, patients and residents have up-to-date estate planning work. That is usually the first time where the estate plan has to start taking effect. These professionals are an excellent referral source and cross-reference because they will usually get feedback after they have referred an attorney.

Go ahead and start to narrow down your search. Refer to the work page at the back of the book to stay organized.

When you finish gathering your names, you will be ready to move to the next step. Try to get a few names. Not just one (Unless you get the same name over and over again. That probably means you're in a small town, or you've found a good one with a reputation for good work).

9. HOW TO ELIMINATE CHOICES

After completing the exercises in the previous chapter, you may have a list of three to five estate planning attorneys from whom you can choose. This chapter will cover how to narrow the list down to one or two attorneys.

The key is to get information about the attorney's law practice and to look over educational materials from that attorney. Now would be a good time to go back and research more on the Internet to hone down which two you think are the best. First, you can always check their attorney site to see if there's any of their personality or the focus of their practice on their website or online videos.

State Bar Website

You should go to www.FloridaBar.org, or your state bar's website for attorney profiles and standing with the Bar. You will want to look at that attorney's profile and see whether or not they've had any bar complaints or professional discipline. Most importantly, you need to make sure the person is a licensed attorney! (That has actually happened with many estate planning scams; there is no licensed attorney involved).

Watch out for how you look up each name. For example, if you try to look me up, you won't find me under the name Kellen Bryant. You'll have to use the name Robert Bryant because Robert is my first name. There is a tool that you can use on the Florida Bar website to search for attorneys by first and last name, and city and state. Other states have similar search functions. From here, you can check to see if they have had any disciplinary action or complaints against them.

Next, pull up the attorney's website again. Most, if not all, attorneys have a list of their credentials on their website. You need to look to see if these are actual credentials that matter to your core estate planning issue. If the attorney has given speeches, written articles, or has appeared in media, you want to make sure that those topics are consistent with your needs. For example, if you want to plan to protect and care for your child with autism, you'll want to see if the attorney has any involvement or has any information on special needs trusts or planning for people who are developmentally disabled.

Conversely, if I need an estate planning attorney to help me with my elderly parents and I find on his or her website that the attorney has written articles about taxes and business planning, then that gives me the indication that that attorney is more of a business succession planning, business asset protection, or estate taxation planning attorney. While excellent in one area, they are not very focused in an area that would provide long-term care for my elderly parent.

Academic Credentials

Another specific thing to look for are the attorney's academic credentials from law school. Grades usually do matter. The attorneys who made good grades in law school will often note them on their website. If you have never heard about law school grades in general, they are very competitive, and only a certain amount of people can make A's. Any attorney who lists that they graduated with honors, high honors, interned with judges, or were part of the moot court, a trial team, or law review, were probably very diligent and excelled in law school. This can translate into being a solid, diligent attorney.

Demographic Information

As you narrow down your search you can also look at what kind of value you place on demographics and age of the attorney. You may decide you want to work with a female attorney versus a male attorney or vice versa. It's all a matter of preference that may matter to you in your happiness and comfort to make sure that this important work is done correctly.

You can also decide if you want an older or younger attorney. If you're working with an older attorney, you may want to consider whether or not that attorney is up to scratch on tips and tricks and latest developments in estate planning, and that they are still involved with conferences, and not just using old tricks. An advantage of a younger attorney is that as your estate planning documents may need to be amended or changed through the years, the young attorney who drafted your estate plan is more likely to be available at his or her law firm. If you work with an older attorney who may retire, you may want to check to see that their successor is someone with whom you will be comfortable working.

Involvement In Specific Groups

When you get to an attorney's website, you may notice that they have an alphabet soup of credentials and involvement in organizations. Some credentials will matter, and some will not.

First and foremost, attorneys who are board certified by their state bar, primarily in the areas of wills, trusts and estates, elder law, and tax may have a good background in estate planning and should be your first lead when searching for an expert attorney to handle your estate plan. You should also look for involvement in estate planning specific groups like WealthCounsel, ElderCounsel, National Network of Estate Planning Attorneys, American

Academy of Estate Planning Attorneys, American College of Trust and Estate Council, Lawyers With Purpose, Academy of V.A. Pension Planners, and so forth.

The main thing you want to look for is an indication that the attorney is involved with groups that focus on *your* particular legal issue at hand. These attorneys will have email networks of other professionals who focus on similar issues. The attorneys can cross-reference with each other about latest trends, what works, and what does not work, so that you can get the best result in your planning. Any of these groups provides their attorney members with software and documents vetted by multiple top experts in the country.

Now you will find recognition based listings such as SuperLawyers®, AVVO, Best Lawyers in America, Martindale-Hubbell (AV® Rated), and so forth. All of these listing are a really good indicator, but the other principles of this book apply, so make sure you determine if the rated lawyers in these groups practice estate planning law in a way that works for you and your needs (because entry onto some of these types of groups and lists can be "gamed".)

Geographic Location

You can narrow down your search by geographic location. Personally, I do not think you should limit yourself to the attorneys who are closest to you. If you look for the closest attorney in geographic relation to your house, you may end up with a general practice attorney or an attorney who does not have a particular focus or specialty for the legal practice area that you need. Don't be afraid to venture outside your suburban area, or even outside your city, as long as you have an attorney who narrowly focuses on the issue that is most important to your estate plan and your wishes.

The key point of this chapter is to narrow down your attorney search. You still may be left with one or two names. A clear winner will come out after your first call and conversation at each attorney's office.

10. OFFICIALLY HIRING AN ATTORNEY

Now you have finished all of your research and have decided upon the attorney who is right for you. This chapter is about what you need to know before you officially start writing checks.

Many people are familiar with how personal injury attorneys are paid for legal services. Usually, as explained in their advertisements, you don't pay a thing unless the attorney wins in court. The attorney takes a cut of the winnings to cover the fees and costs of your case. Estate planning attorneys do not work that way and should not work that way. Estate planning attorneys can either work on an hourly basis or a flat fee basis.

How much will it cost?

A couple of general factors will affect your total attorney fee, whether or not you pay by the hour or one flat fee:

Your location. Downtown attorneys may cost more because they have more overhead, or are a large law firm. Rural attorneys may cost less because they operate differently and have less overhead. Attorneys in the north may charge less than attorneys in other areas of the country because of the cost of living.

Your net worth. If you have $10 million and up, estate taxes are a big issue in your estate plan. Proper planning can save you millions of dollars in taxes. This type of estate plan costs more because of the complication involved, the level of education the attorney needs (these attorneys require an additional Master's degree in tax law), and the level of risk to the law firm in instances of malpractice. Accordingly, attorney fees can easily hit five-figures in these cases.

The type of assets you own. More complicated assets cost more in estate planning costs. Which sounds easier to work with: (a) $500,000 consisting of 3 rental properties, 2 cash value life insurance policies, an oil well in Mississippi, and stock at 3 different companies; versus (b) $500,000 in a money market account at one bank. If your estate sounds like (a), then expect to pay more to get your planning done right.

Your goals. If you have $10 million and do not care that your family may have to pay millions in estate taxes, then you can get a basic durable power of attorney, will, and health directives for under $1,000, easy. Alternatively, if you have $150,000 and you want to pass it to your adult child with a disability without

75

affecting her Medicaid-based group home services, then you could pay fees exceeding $3,000 in some areas. Your goals increase complexity, increase ultimate value to you and your estate, and thus affect cost.

Speed of completion. Are you going on an overseas vacation next week and want this all done? Is your family calling for an attorney to meet you in the hospital for emergency planning? You're going to pay extra for jumping ahead of the line, attorney travel time, and for the malpractice risk to the attorney.

The type of attorney. General practice attorneys will charge less, specialists charge more. Who charges more in medicine: the family practice physician or the brain surgeon?

Trust based plans versus will based plans. If your estate involves a trust agreement, then you will pay more than if your plan involves only a will. A trust takes more time to set up properly and explain.

Controlling beyond the grave. There are two basic ways to give your family money when you pass: 1) they get a check and do what they want with it; or 2) you provide them their inheritance in a trust that has rules in stipulations. The trust provides asset protection from creditors, divorces, bankruptcy, and in general money mismanagement. You can even say that the kids do not get the money until X, Y, and Z occur. Option #2 costs more.

What Will I Get For the Fee?

First of all, you need to know what your estate plan will include. You must always remember you are buying advice and the documents implement the advice.

It may seem obvious, but sometimes if you ask for a will, you will only get a will. Many times you also need such things as a financial power of attorney, and healthcare advanced directives. Be clear about whether you want a complete, comprehensive plan, or you just want one document, which could leave you vulnerable in other spots.

What Fees May Be Included In Creation of a Trust?

After you have educated yourself and consulted with your attorney, you may decide that you want to put some of your assets into a trust. Estate planning attorneys may charge differently when it comes to setting up a trust account. After the trust is created, there is an administrative process required to change the names of your accounts, real estate, and other assets. This process will transfer them into a trust account. Some attorneys will do this administrative work for you and charge you for their time. Some will give you the option to transfer the assets yourself to avoid the extra fee. It's important to talk to your attorney about what exactly they expect payment for so that there are no surprises.

In addition to the administrative work needed to set up a trust, there are other aspects of estate planning in which an attorney may delegate work to others and work with a team. He or she may have a partner, associate attorney, or paralegals who help to draft your documents. The one basic thing to look out for is hourly billing for each team member drafting your documents. It would be unnecessary, for example, to pay a team of four attorneys to talk about your case and draft your documents unless you have well over $50 million. Most estate planning work should be handled in smaller teams and should not require a group of attorneys billing unless you specifically permit it. Other team members may work on your estate, such as a paralegal. This should be fine as long as the final product meets your needs, and should not constitute any abnormal billing. Talk to your attorney about who will handle the different stages of your estate plan and how payments will be made.

Will There Be Any Ongoing Fees?

The last thing you should determine is whether there will be any ongoing fees after your estate plan is complete. You should discuss what the attorney's policy is on document updates. You should be very clear on whether the attorney offers an annual maintenance fee based plan. Many attorneys will charge a flat fee annually for this service, and you should decide if it is something that interests you. Once the attorney knows your family situation and has created your plan, he or she should be able to update your documents fairly easily and recommend what is best for your estate plan. Many estate planning documents include a high level of contingency planning, which provides "back-up" plans in your documents. Contingencies usually mean that you will need to update your will less frequently due to changes in your family situation or financial situation. When updates are needed, the process will be much simpler, especially if you use the same attorney.

In addition, you should also consider asking the attorney who will do the updates. Some attorneys will update all documents themselves, which can be problematic if the updates are simple enough for a paralegal to do. You do not want to pay too much for a very small change.

CONCLUSIONS

- With an estate plan you buy advice, not just documents. Documents are a means in which your advice is implemented.

- Some providers give minimal advice and education, others are more specialized and comprehensive in their planning. The more educational components an attorney offers in his or her process, the more prepared you will be to work with them, and you'll get the most out of every dollar you spend.

- You need to find an attorney who's law practice focuses on your core estate planning issue

- Some providers provide minimal planning for a high fee. Make sure you pay less for your plan when you expect to get less in return.

- The ideal estate plan should include the Perfect Planning Triangle so that you get what you need for you and your family at the best price.

- When it comes to estate plans, you get what you pay for. A bad provider can cause more problems than they solve.

MY CORE ESTATE PLANNING ISSUE:

Attorney Name	1.	2.	3.
Practice Areas:			
Professional Reference or Cross-Reference:			
Notes from Attorney Website			
Educational Materials and Information offered:			
Online Rating System			
State Bar Profile			

R. KELLEN BRYANT

ABOUT THE AUTHOR

Kellen Bryant is the founder of Law Office of R. Kellen Bryant, P.L. and a Jacksonville, Florida native. Kellen focuses his law practice on estate planning and elder law with a particular focus on asset protection and preservation from long term care costs, creditors, and predators. If you would like additional information about the estate planning and elder care law topics discussed in this book, you can go to www.kellenbryantlaw.com

www.ingramcontent.com/pod-product-compliance
Lightning Source LLC
Chambersburg PA
CBHW071724170526
45165CB00005B/2138